Colonel Juan Batista de Anza, governor of New Mexico; diary of his expedition to the Moquis in 1780; paper read before the Historical society at its annual meeting, 1918. With an introduction and notes by Ralph E. Twitchell

Juan Bautista de Anza, Ralph Emerson Twitchell

HISTORICAL SOCIETY

OF

NEW MEXICO

No. 21

Colonel Juan Bautista de Anza
Governor of New Mexico
Diary of his Expedition to the Moquis in 1780

Paper read before the Historical Society at its
Annual Meeting, 1918.

With an Introduction and Notes by
RALPH E. TWITCHELL
Vice-President of the Historical
Society of New Mexico

PUBLICATIONS OF THE SOCIETY

No 1.—1881—Inaugural Address of Hon W. G Ritch. 20 pp.

No. 2 —1882—"Kin and Clan," by Adolph F Bandelier 8 pp.

No. 3 —1896—"The Stone Idols of New Mexico" (Illustrated) 17 pp.

No 4.—1903—"The Stone Lions of Cochiti," by Hon. L. Bradford Prince

No. 5.—1904—Bi-ennial Report, English 13 pp

No 6 —1904—Bi-ennial Report, Spanish 13 pp

No. 7 —1906—"The Franciscan Martyrs of 1680" 28 pp.

No 8.—1906—The Defeat of the Comanches in 1716 By Hon. Amado Chaves. 9 pp.

No. 9.—1907—Bi-ennial Report

No. 10 —1907—Journal of New Mexico Convention of September, 1849 22 pp

No. 11 —1908—The California Column. (Illustrated) By Capt George H. Pettis. 45 pp.

No 12.—1908—Carson's Fight with the Comanches at Adobe Walls. By Capt. George H. Pettis. 35 pp

No 13 —1909—Bi-ennial Report. 13 pp

No. 14 —1909—The Palace, Santa Fe, N. M (8 pp. Edition, 2,500)

No. 15 —1910—Catalogue of Books in the Library of the Society, relating to New Mexico and the Southwest (English.) 49 pp

No 16.—1911—"The Spanish Language in New Mexico and Southern Colorado," by Aurélio M. Espinosa, Ph. D 37 pp

No 17 —1912—Official Report, 1909 to 1911

No 18.—1913—Official Report, 1912.

No 19.—1914—Official Report, 1912 and 1913

NO. 20.—1917—Historical Sketch of Governor William Carr Lane, by Ralph E. Twitchell. pp 62.

HISTORICAL SOCIETY

OF

NEW MEXICO

—

No. 21

—

Colonel Juan Bautista de Anza
Governor of New Mexico
Diary of his Expedition to the Moquis in 1780

—

Paper read before the Historical Society at its
Annual Meeting, 1918.

—

With an Introduction and Notes by
RALPH E. TWITCHELL
Vice-President of the Historical
Society of New Mexico

From Painting by Vierra—Courtesy State Museum.

OLD MISSION AT PUEBLO OF SANTA ANA.

Colonel Juan Bautista de Anza

Governor of New Mexico

Diary of His Expedition to the Moquis in 1780, with an Introduction and Notes.

GREAT leaders, whether in war or in peace, have always been men endowed with some peculiar fitness, some quality of genius; but the countries they have governed, the armies they have commanded, or the movements they have sponsored or led, have been successful because the average leader, be he soldier or civilian, has always, in a lesser or greater degree, exhibited the simple qualities of loyalty, courage and patriotism.

These characteristics have been notably in evidence in the careers and accomplishments of some of the governors and captains-general of New Mexico

The American of average education is more or less familiar with the exploits and achievements of French and English colonial executives It is only in recent years, however, that much attention, other than that given to the most celebrated of the Spanish rulers in America, has been given to those representatives of old Spain, who guided the destinies of the areas now under American sovereignty.

During the 18th and 19th centuries we can not say that much was done in aid of the material prosperity of our section of Spanish America; but the Spanish government, through the courage and loyalty of its official representatives, did dig deep, preparing the foundations of the present great southwestern and far-western states of the American union.[1]

---

1 **Early Explorations of Father Garcés on the Pacific.Slope;** Herbert E. Bolton, The Pacific Ocean in History, McMillan Company, New York, 1917
"It is the popular opinion in the country at large, inculcated by unin-

No country is secure in its future unless the substructure is cemented in business energy and enterprise, nor has any nation ever remained great, if the people placed sole reliance upon material prosperity The insistent, fighting spirit of the Crusader, the conqueror of primeval forest and desert expanse, the hardihood of the explorer, the prowess and fortitude of the pathfinder and the trail-blazer, the unswerving character of the apostle of beliefs and principles, must always be present and prepared for any adventure, if a nation shall remain permanent in its greatness. It is on this account that a more lasting recognition is due and is always accorded to those figures in history whose vision sensed the future of a race and nation.

In this section of Spanish America, in the period of which we write, no matter what may have been the vision of the Spaniard, destiny had already affixed its seal. The great southwest and California, in less than a century were to become a part of the mighty republic, whose foundations were then being laid by Samuel Adams, John Hancock and Benjamin Franklin.

In two centuries of English colonial government the influences and accompaniments of nineteenth century civilization had barely crossed the Alleghenies. The Frenchman and the Spaniard had traversed the valley of the Mississippi and in some parts of the interior had established forts and maintained garrisons and Indian trading posts; but, in our section, the intrepid cávalier, with small armies and limited supplies, had pushed far to the north, more than a thousand five hundred miles, encountered savage hordes, traversed the mountain and plain, pacified the various peoples, and for more than a hundred and fifty years had built towns and cities, erected king-

formed writers of school histories, that Spanish activities within the present limits of the United States reached their climax with the founding of St. Augustine and Santa Fe. The fact is, however, that from 1519 to the opening of the nineteenth century, Spain continued steadily to extend her frontiers northward, and that the last third of the eighteenth century was a period of as great advance as any other of equal length after the death of Cortés This activity involved not only the founding of new missions and settlements and the occupation of new military outposts, but embraced also an extensive series of explorations quite as vast and important for territory now within the United States as the earlier expeditions ... . as late as 1769 the interior of Alta California was practically unknown, the California coast had not been run by a recorded exploration since Vizcaíno, the Utah Basin was all but untrod by white man, the trail from Santa Fe to the Missouri had been little used by Spaniards since 1720, the whole northern half of Texas was almost unknown to recorded exploration, and direct communication had never been established between Santa Fe and San Antonio, or between El Paso and San Antonio.

doms and capitals and established the sovereignty of the crown, claiming to the east as far as the Mississippi and to the frozen regions of the north.

Always anticipating and jealous of possible encroachments by the French and English upon the northern provinces of New Spain, by virtue of a royal mandate of August 22, 1776, the northern and northwestern provinces of Mexico were formed with a new and distinct organization, called the Internal Provinces of New Spain. This organization included California. It conferred ample powers, civil, military and political upon the commandant-general.[2] Until December 4, 1786, New Spain was divided into ten kingdoms or provinces, which were: New Mexico, New Galicia, New Leon, New Santander, Texas, Coahuila, New Biscay, Sonora, Sinaloa and Upper and Lower California The Cavallero de Croix was the first commandant-general He soon petitioned the crown to divide his territory, but no action was taken until 1786, when, by royal order, New Biscay and New Mexico were placed under a commandant-inspector, and Coahuila and Texas under Don Juan Ugalde, the commandant-general having charge of Sonora and the Californias and exercising general supervision over the whole of the Provincias Internas.[3]

Several years prior to the organization of the Provincias Internas, under orders from the viceroy at the City of Mexico, an expedition was organized in four divisions, two by land and two by sea, for the purpose of occupying Upper California and fortifying the ports of San Diego and Monterey. This expedition was commanded by Don Gaspar de Portolá, a captain of dragoons and governor of the Californias.

At this time, there was stationed at the presidio of Tubac, in northern Sonora, now a part of the state of Arizona, Don

2 Ten years later authority was given to the governor of California by the commandant-general at Chihuahua to make grants of land, limiting the number of sitios which could be legally granted. In 1792, California was annexed to the vice-royalty of Mexico and so continued until the Spanish authority ceased United States v Peralta, 19 Howard, 347
3 These kingdoms or provinces were at that time divided into forty-two districts, called alcaldías mayores—a territorial division under a chief alcalde
New Mexico was never placed under an intendancy when the changes were made in 1786, but remained under the Commandancia See Hall's Mexican Law, secs. 12-15
The viceroy and the commandant-general possessed about the same powers and exercised the same functions In 1788, regulations were made by the viceroy by the terms of which the commandant-general—the successor of Cavallero de Croix, Ugarte y Loyola, remained in command of the Californias, Sonora, New Mexico and New Biscay. The commandant had no fixed residence but traveled from place to place

New Mexico Historical Society Collections.

PUEBLO OF SAN FELIPE.

Juan Bautista de Anza, captain and commandant of the garrison. He manifested a lively interest in the expedition commanded by Captain Portolá and requested of the viceroy that he be permitted to lead an expedition at his own cost from Tubac to Monterey by way of the Gila and Colorado rivers, joining the Portolá command at Monterey His petition was denied and the Portolá expedition founded the presidios of San Diego and Monterey and at the same time the celebrated missions of San Diego, Monterey, San Antonio, San Gabriel and San Luis Obispo

In the course of time it was demonstrated that if a line of communication by land from Sonora to the Coast could be established, it would be most profitable as the transportation of supplies by sea had proven very unsatisfactory

Captain de Anza therefore renewed his petition to take an expedition overland to Monterey at his own expense. The matter was placed before the crown by the viceroy and in time the king directed that the desired permission not only be given but that the royal treasury should bear the expense.

Captain de Anza made his preparations with military promptness and, on January 8th, 1774, set out with two padres,[4] an escort of twenty soldiers, some guides, thirty-four persons in all and one hundred and forty saddle and pack animals and sixty-five head of beef cattle. After many vicissitudes, he succeeded in reaching, on March 22, the mission of San Gabriel, and later, on April 18, the presidio of Monterey, where he was most joyfully received. He returned by way of the Colorado river, crossing at Yuma, and reaching Tubac on May 27, 1774

Captain de Anza was the first military officer, then, to

4 Fray Dias and Fray Francisco Hermenejildo Garcés, a Franciscan missionary of the College of Santa Cruz de Queretaro "After the expulsion of the Jesuits from Pimeria Alta in 1767" says Bolton. op cit. p 318, "fourteen Queretarans were sent to take their places Among them was Father Garcés, who was assigned to the mission of San Xavier del Bac, then and still standing nine miles south of Tucson It was his position at this northernmost outpost, combined with his rare personal qualities that brought him into prominence in the new wave of frontier advance His principal contributions to the explorations of the period were (1) to reopen the trails made by Kino, Keller and Sedelmayr, to the Gila and through the Papagueria, (2) to serve as pathfinder across the Yuma and Colorado deserts, and as guide for Ansa to the foot of the San Jacinto Mountains, when he led the first overland expedition from Sonora to California, and (3) to discover a way from Yuma to New Mexico, and across the Mojave desert to Los Angeles and the Tulares, and between these two points by way of the Tejon Pass Altogether his pathfinding, accomplished without the aid of a single white man, covered more than a thousand miles of untrod trails, and furnished an example of physical endurance and human courage that have rarely been excelled"

conquer the desert in an overland route to Upper California. He had demonstrated that a route by land was practicable and on his return to New Spain, he visited the City of Mexico when he was promoted to the grade of lieutenant-colonel and commissioned to form a company of soldiers and conduct an expedition to Monterey, from which point they were to operate in the further enterprise of establishing a presidio and mission at San Francisco.[5]

The second expedition was organized at San Felipe de Sinaloa and headquarters were established at San Miguel de Horcasitas, at that time the residence of the governor of Sonora By royal order the entire expense of the expedition was born by the crown, even to the extent of clothing and equipping the entire party of colonists. One hundred and forty pack-mules were required to transport the supplies. There were one hundred and twenty horses and twenty-five mules for the use of the soldiers, two hundred and twenty horses for the expedition and three hundred and twenty head of live stock for its maintenance and the aid of the establishments which had been installed on the Rio Colorado and in California. The commander took with him the ensign, sergeant and eight private soldiers from Tubac and enlisted twenty additional; there were four families of settlers, all of whom received pay and rations. In charge of the spiritual welfare of the expedition and for educational and missionary work among the In-

5 Dr Herbert E Bolton, working in the Mexican Archives between 1903 and 1908 discovered much material dealing with the explorations made by Fr Garcés between the years 1770 and 1776, although portions in less complete form had been known and examined by Bancroft, Eldredge and others The material brought to light by Bolton is as follows (1) Diary of Fr. Garcés of his expedition of 1770 (Diario que se ha formado por el Viage hecho á el Rio Gila quando los Yndios Pimas Gileños me llamararon á fin de que baptisase sus hijos que estaban enfermos del Saramplon); (2) Diary of Fr Garcés of his expedition of 1771 (Diario que se ha formado con la ocasion de la entrada que hize á los vecinos Gentiles); (3) Diary of Fr Garcés of his expedition of 1774 (Diario de la entrada que se practica de orden del Exmo. Sr. Vi Rey Dn. Antonio Maria Bucarely y Ursua producida en Junta de Guerra i real acienda de abrir camino por los rios Gila y Colorado para los nuebos establecimientos de San Diego y Monte Rey, etc) (4) Diaries of the 1774 expedition by Ansa and Father Juan Diaz (Diario, que forma el Padre Fr. Juan Diaz Missionero Appco. del Colegio de la Sta Cruz de Queretaro, en el viage, que hace en compañia del R. P. Fr. Franco Garcés para abrir camino desde la Provincia de la Sonora a la California Septentrional, y puerto de Monterrey por los Rios y Colorado, etc.) (5) A summary by Fr Garcés of his first four expeditions (Copia de las noticias sacadas, y remitidas por el Pe. Predicador Fr. Franco Garcés de los Diarios que ha formado en las quatro entradas practicadas desde el año de 68 hasta el presente de 75 á la frontera septentrinal de los Gentiles de Nueva Espana) (6) Report by Fr. Garcés to Fray Diego Ximénez. in Copia de barios Papeles del R. P. Fr. Franco Garcés, Missionero en la Pimeria alta. (7) A great quantity of correspondence of Garcés, Ansa, Díaz and others relating to the general question of northward expansion from Sonora between 1768 and 1776, of which Garcés' explorations formed a part

dians, there were three frayles—Pedro Font, Francisco Garcés and Tomás Esaire, the last two accompanying the expedition as far as the Rio Colorado where they remained teaching the Indians pending the return of Colonel de Anza from Monterey and the site of the new presidio of San Francisco [6]

In all there were two hundred and forty soldiers, colonists, men, women and children in the expedition. The start for Tubac was made in September, 1775. A muster was had on the afternoon of September 29th, at 4:30, and immediately thereafter the march across the mountains and desert of Apacheland was begun.[7] It was not until late in October that Tubac[8] was reached, and the 23rd of that month the march to Upper California was resumed. Their route lay to the north, passing the mission of San Xavier del Bac,[9] the site of the present city of Tucson and thence to the river Gila, near the site of the Casa Grande, which they visited Their course now lay down the Gila to its junction with the Colorado, which they reached on November 20th, where the expedition was joyfully received by Salvador Palma, chief of the Yuma tribe. Colonel De Anza now sent out parties for the purpose of ascertaining some ford in the river, and finally located a place where the river ran in three parts and not deeper than four feet and about 850 feet in width On November 30th the river

6. "The relation of Garcés' undertaking to the Ansa expedition and to the opening of an overland route from Sonora to Los Angeles is especially important In 1769, according to Palou, Ansa had offered to undertake the task, but was not encouraged But the return of Garcés brought the matter to a head After talking with Garces, on May 2, 1772, Anza renewed his proposal, using as his principal argument the information which Garcés had acquired. He emphasized the fact (1) that the Indians where Garcés had been told of white men not far beyond, and whom they had seen; (2) that beyond the Colorado river Garcés had discovered a Sierra Madre, hitherto unseen from the East, but which must be that beyond which was San Diego, (3) that the desert was much narrower than had been supposed, and the difficulties from lack of water therefore much less "In view of this," he continued, "this Reverend Father and I concluded that the distance to Monte Rey is not so enormous as used to be estimated, and that it will not be impossible to compass it " He closed by requesting that if the plan should be approved Father Garcés might be permitted to go with him " Bolton, op. cit p 329

7   There was a delay in the start owing to the fact that an escort of soldiers from Tubac to Horcasitas had the misfortune to lose all of their horses in a surprise attack by the Apaches.

8. Tubac was located in the southern part of Arizona, on the Santa Cruz river, about forty miles south of Tucson, near the present Mexican boundary

9   San Xavier del Bac was the most northern of the missions in what is now the state of Arizona, it was established subsequent to the re-conquest by General Don Diego de Vargas, probably in 1697 See Mange's Diary of Fr Kino's journey in 1699 The present city of Tucson was founded in the year following de Ansa's 2nd expedition to Upper California, 1776, when the presidio of Tubac was moved to that place which was then called San Agustin de Tucson Fr Garcés had been in charge of this Mission since 1768

New Mexico Historical Society Collections.

PUEBLO OF LAGUNA.

was crossed on rafts, with no injury to any member of the expedition other than the wetting of their clothes.[10]

In this paper space will not permit a recital of the many experiences and events of the journey from this point to Monterey and the site of the new presidio which was to be established. The entire diary of the expedition should be translated and annotated. It is sufficient here to state that the presidio of Monterey was reached on the morning of April 8th, 1776. On the 14th of April, he began his return march to Sonora, taking with him from Yuma, on his arrival at the Rio Colorado, Salvador Palma, the Yuma chief, his brother Pablo, and another Indian. They reached San Miguel de Horcasitas on June 1st, 1776. Colonel de Anza now proceeded to the City of Mexico accompanied by the Yuma chief and his brother. The entire party were entertained by the Viceroy and lived with Colonel de Anza at his residence in the Calle de Merced. The Indians were baptized and the viceroy presented Palma with a captain's staff.[11]

Colonel de Anza remained in the City of Mexico for a considerable period but not later than 1777, for in that year he had returned to the command of the presidio of Tubac, now removed to San Agustin de Tucson, having already been rewarded for his great undertaking in establishing overland communication with the California presidios and missions, with a commission as governor of the province or kingdom of New Mexico.

Colonel de Anza succeeded Don Pedro Fermin de Mendinueta as governor of New Mexico, having been appointed to the office in June of that year. He did not assume the duties of the office at Santa Fe until late in 1778, probably in the month of July.[12]

10   The diary recites that the tallest and strongest horses were used by the women and children of the expedition in fording the river, accompanied by ten men on the lower side, so that they could be saved in case of a fall into the river. Fr Garcés was carried across on the backs of three Yuma Indians, two at his head and one at his feet
11   This was according to a custom and policy of the Spanish officials. Many Comanche chiefs held commissions as "captains" and "generals" in the Spanish army
12   The Spanish Archives of New Mexico, R E Twitchell, 1914. Vol II, p. 260, Archive No 720: Cavallero de Croix, Chihuahua, February 11, 1778 Letter to the governor of New Mexico, requesting him to come to Chihuahua, leaving the government in the hands of the Captain, Francisco Trebol Navarro ad interim; stating that his successor, Colonel Juan Bautista de Anza, was still detained in Sonora Ibid, p 261, Archive No 724: Pedro Fermin de Mendinueta, Santa Fe, March 10, 1778 Bando, giving notice of the appointment of Francisco Trebol Navarro as governor ad interim and of his own departure for Chihuahua Ibid, p 262, Archive 734; Pedro

During the first year of de Anza's rule he ordered the taking of a census and the making of a map of the province, which was accomplished, the map and census returns being regularly forwarded to the commandancia at Chihuahua.[13] He organized and personally led an expedition against the Comanche nation, his force consisting of 645 men, 85 of which

Fermin de Mendinueta, Chihuahua, June 22, 1778   Detallo de Servicio to be followed in the Province of New Mexico   A certified copy of document sent from Chihuahua to the acting governor, Trebol Navarro   Ibid, p 264, Archive No 751; Juan Bautista de Anza, Santa Fe, December 30. 1778 Notizia del Armamento etc pertaining to the government of New Mexico received by him, with notes from 1779 to 1781

13. This map was made by Don Bernardo Miera y Pacheco, an officer of engineers who had served at the post at El Paso and at Santa Fe   He emigrated from Chihuahua to New Mexico, arriving at El Paso in 1744 He was accompanied by his wife, Doña Rumualda Vialpando, and one son, Cleto   From the time of his arrival at El Paso until 1768, as he states in Archive No. 582, Twitchell op cit vol. I, "he was ready for all and everything that has been required of me in the royal service " He accompanied the Frayles Atanasio Dominguez and Francisco Sylvestre Escalante, in 1776, from Santa Fe, on their journey to the Pacific Coast for the purpose of discovering "A route from the Presidio of Santa Fe, New Mexico, to Monterrey in Southern California " He made a map of that journey The year previous he had accompanied Fr Escalante to Moqui and made a map of that route.   He also made a map of the Villa of Santa Fe which was used by de Anza in his plans for the re-building of the presidio at Santa Fe See Archive 814, op. cit, p 285, Presidio of Santa Fe, January 19, 1781 Instructions relative to a plan for a new presidio according to the plans of Don Geronimo de la Rocha y Figueroa, etc

See Descriptive List of Maps of Spanish Possessions, etc Lowery Coll. Library of Congress, p 377 Map of Moqui Province Ms 21.3x30 cms Unsigned, undated   Original in Acad de la Hist Madrid Col Boturini, to 25. bet fols 318-319 It accompanies the "Informe y Diario de la entrada que en Junio de 1775 hizo á la Provincia de Moqui el P Predic Fr Silvestre Velez Escalante testimoniado por el Secretario de Provincia M R P Fernando Antonio Gomez," ibid, fols Curious Gives the different villages of the group with the number of families in each

Also at p 390, op. cit Plano Geografico de la Tierra descubierta, nuevamente, á los Rumbos Norte Noroeste y Oeste, del Nuevo Mexico demarcado por mi Don Bernardo de Miera y Pacheco que entró a hacer su descubrimiento en compañia de los R Rs P Ps fr. Francisco Atanacio Domingues y Fr Silbestre Vclestre Veles [Escalante] segun consta en el Diario y Derrotero que se hizo y se Remitio á S M por mano de su Virrei con Plano á la lettra; El que dedica Al Sr. D Teodoro de la Croix del Insigne Orden Teutonica Comandante General en Gefe de Lima y Provincias de esta America Septentrional por S M. hecho en S. Phe el Real de Chiguagua. Año de 1778 Ms 81.3x66 5 cms   2 vignettes in color

Original in Brit Mus Add Ms 17 661-D Includes 31 degrees 30 minutes to 42 degrees 30 minutes North Lat and 261 degrees to 273 degrees Long (from Teneriffe)   "It is by another hand than the Domingues map," says Lowery, but I doubt it.

Also at p. 384, op. cit. Plano geografico, de la tierra descubierta, y demarcada por Dn Bernardo de Miera, y Pacheco al Rumbo del Noroeste y Oeste del Nuevo Mexico, quien fue en compañia de los RRs. P. Ps fr franco. Atanacio Domingues, Uisitador, Comisario y Custodio de esta, y fr Silvestre Velez de Escalante, siendo uno del numero de las diez personas que acompañaron á dhós R. Rs Padres, como constará en el Diario Derrotero que hicieron á que se remite en todo, con el fin unico del servicio de ambas Magestades, el que va adjunto en dicho Diario al Comandante General de las Provincias Internas el Sor Brigadier de los Rs Exercitos Cavallero Croix, á quien humilde y rendidamente dedican esta pequeña obra, por la Direcion del Coronel Dn Pedro fermin de Mendinueta Governador de este Reyno, para los fines que pueden conducir al bien de tantas Almas que sean ser Christianas, y al servicio de Nuestro Catholico Soberano Ms. 81x70 cms Unsigned, undated

Original in Dep de la Guerra. Madrid Arch. de Mapas. L M. 8a-Ia-a No. 40 Extends from 35 degrees N. Lat. to 42 degrees N Lat. and from 272 degrees to 262 degrees West, i e from a litle east of Rio del Norte to 200 or 300 miles west of the Colorado Shows New Mexico north of Isleta and Acoma, Moqui Province with several village names, sources of Colorado river & etc. Very interesting.

were soldiers, the others being vecinos[14] and Indians. Leaving Santa Fe he marched to the north and northeast a distance of ninety-five leagues, engaging in battle a large number of Comanches under the leadership of Cuerno Verde, a famous chief who was killed as were also four of his subordinate chiefs, his principal medicine-man, his oldest son and thirty-two warriors.[15]

Governor de Anza visited all of the pueblo villages of his province, took steps looking to a re-building of the Santa Fe presidio,[16] concentrated some of the missions, and engaged in almost constant warfare with the hostile tribes

Not the least important of the many events of de Anza's rule was his visit to the province of Moqui in 1780, of which expedition he kept a diary,[17] a complete translation of which, with the accompanying papers, is as follows:—

"The Commandant General of the Interior Provinces of New Spain· Sends copy of the latest proceedings in the Dispatch concerning the Reduction of the Moquis

Esteemed Sir:—

In my letter N. 476 of the 23d of February '80, I gave Your Excellency an account of the deplorable state in which the Moqui Indians were found, of the lucky and opportune occasion for conquering them and of my efforts directed to that end. In Paragraphs 136 to 140 of the First Part of the General Report which accompanied Letter No 735, I reported the results of all these things, and in this I enclose a Copy of the latest proceedings in the Dispatch, it being confirmed by the official letter in which the Governor of New Mexico, Don Juan Bautista de Anza, makes evident the obduracy of the Moquis, and their inevitable extermination by the ravages of the epidemic of smallpox and the war upon them waged by the Utes and Navajos, notwithstanding de Anza is endeavoring to do them all possible good in order to attract the remainder of the unhappy Moqui Nation to a knowledge of the true faith and the mild rule of the King all of which I beg Your Excellency will be pleased to have presented to His Majesty.

---

14. Militia.
15 Anza, Juan Bautista, Diario de la Expedicion que sale á practicar Contra la nacion Comancha, 1779, Ms N. Mex. Doc 861-922.
16 The presidio was not rebuilt until the rule of Governor Fernando de la Concha in 1791.
17 General Archives of the Indies, Seville (Audiencia de Guad 104-6-19) Doc 187. No. 738 The original of the Diario was in the Santa Fe Archives

New Mexico Historical Society Collections.

OLD MISSION CHURCH AT LAGUNA.

Our Lord keep Your Excellency many years   Arispe 23d
of April, 1782

Esteemed sir   Your most attached and faithful servant
kisses your hand.

(RUBRIC)   CAVro DE CROIX.

To Honorable Señor Don Joseph de Galvez '''18
Señor Governor and Commandant General —

My Dear Sir —By your Excellency's Superior order of
the 31st December of last year, I received the Copies of the
Royal Orders of Feb. 14, 1777, and Feb. 20, 1779, by which I
am made acquainted with the pious, Christian and fixed rules
by which His Majesty desires that the Indians be treated; not
only those who wish to submit to him as vassals, but also those
who have declared war upon us; from which sovereign purposes my conduct shall not depart in everything that may present itself on this Point-since in their execution and punctual
fulfillment I shall enjoy the success that I desire

In consequence of this, and my anxiety for what Your
Excellency ordered me to do in the matter of transferring my
self to the Province of Moqui, I sent to those Natives, immediately upon the receipt of the Orders indicated, safe and
faithful Emissaries to inform them that I am ready to go and
lead them to those Pueblos at any time they may wish to come
and establish themselves in them. which result I hope to accomplish, if they make favorable reply: in which case, I
shall carry into effect all that Your Honor orders on this
Point, not intending to do so without this preliminary, because, although it is certain that the great and continually in-
creasing Calamities of hunger and Pestilence have depopulated
the most of this Province, as confirmed reports assure me,
it is also true that, in general, there exists the same hostility
as before against submitting themselves to us.

Notwithstanding this, by the Favor of Heaven, I did succeed in having conducted seventy-seven persons at one time,
with the same diligence previously shown in the month of
February of this year; with them, Rev. Father Fray Andrés
Garcia, to whom I had committed this expedition, arrived at

until recent years   It is now in the so-called **Pinart Collection** in California
It was undoubtedly **stolen** while in the collection at Santa Fe
    18   In 1779 Arispe was made the capital of Sonora   **Archive No** 782,
op cit p 281

this Villa on the 20th of March, not having succeeded in se-
curing a larger number owing to lack of means.

These persons have established themselves in the Pueblos
selected by themselves, where I have had given to them the
same favors, gifts and privileges as are enjoyed by their own
residents, and the latter have undertaken to maintain them at
their own expense for this year on account of the benefit re-
sulting to them by this increase of people, who are living in
their new stations very contentedly, without longing to return to their old country, their number having already increased to one hundred and fifty—in which are included twenty to twenty-five dead—; all of them have had the benefit of
the Water of Baptism and with the condition of having been
born in such rebelliousness, not one has failed to ask for it,
when he learned the necessity for this succor

"We could have secured a larger number of the aforesaid,
but we should have found ourselves opposed by the Navajo
Nation at the place half-way between here and Moqui; because
they had massacred and made prisoners of two parties of these
unfortunates who were seeking our care and protection Other parties, for the same reason, were so intimidated that they
gave up and suspended carrying out the second expedition and
others which might have followed.

"So for this and also for various insults in the way of
thefts, although small ones, I have demanded that this Nation
shall observe the capitulations under which peace was granted
them. At El Paso, they excused their bad conduct with base-
less pretexts; they do not make amends, and, therefore, I in-
tend to strike terror in them in the Persons of their Allies,
the Gila Apaches, as I have declared in another communication of the same date—No. 139

' This last plan can only be frustrated by a great raid o
Comanches, or, if it is necessary for me to proceed to the
Province of Moqui, I shall satisfy myself whether this is necessary in order to secure the results commensurate with the enterprise, because, if not, I shall continue to make use of the
means that I have used until now—that of going and coaxing
them in small parties.

"Therefore, for these, as also for the larger (party) that
I mention—conducted by Rev Father Fray Andrés Garcia, I

have released some horses from among those which I have in this fort as re-mounts; there have been some losses among them owing to the great distances and the severity of the weather; to which I have added other helps in provisions, tobacco and some other little gifts to please those converted, the cost of which I have met myself; and, having no order by which to-draw upon what may be expended in the future among these natives, as well as among the other pagan nations who make some recognition of us and remain quiet, I beseech Your Excellency to be pleased to inform me in what way and manner this may be settled in the future.

"The last news coming to me as to the condition of the Moquis is that the majority of them are taking shelter with the Coriña Nation—one of those inhabiting the Rio Colorado—in order to enjoy the fruits of such crops of corn and wheat as may be planted there, whence they assure me they are inclined to remove all those who do not join us, in case it should so happen that they have no rain this present year, as in previous years, because it is impossible for them to continue to live in their old pueblos owing to the lack of seed of every sort, and even stock, which was abundant, since they assure me that the many thousands of sheep are now reduced to a few hundreds, because they ceased caring for them as before, so that they could join themselves with the Apaches.

"This information, with that preceding, is called to Your Excellency's attention in order that you may be pleased to give me orders concerning it all.

"May Our Lord keep Your Excellency many years. Sta Fee, May 26, 1780. B. S. M. Your most devoted and faithful servant kisses your hand.

JUAN BAUPTᴬ DE ANZA

"To Señor Mariscal de Campo Teodoro de Croix

"Arispe 22 July 1780".

"To the Counsellor with the preceeding papers--Decroix--

"Señor Commandant-General:

The Lieutenant-Colonel and Governor of New Mexico, Don Juan Bautista de Anza, after having given an account of the unhappy condition to which the lack of rains has reduced the Moquis; the effect produced by the proceedings for inducing them to submit and join the settlements in those provinces

Courtesy State Museum—Otero Collections.
PUEBLO OF ZUNI.

of the number he has succeeded in gathering up and reuniting, which would have been much greater had they not been prevented by the Navajos capturing and destroying two bands who were going to the same destination, and frightening the others who were disposed and resolved to do so; he shows that in order to aid, satisfy and remove them, he has released some horses from among those he had in reserve at the Fort, and on account of the distance and the severity of the weather some losses resulted; and also that he has given provisions, tobacco and other small gifts, which he paid for out of his own salary; and having no orders or means with which to meet these expenses and those which in the future may arise in his efforts to attract this nation, as well as to the making of gifts to other pagans who give us some recognition and remain at peace, he asks that Your Excellency be pleased to say in what manner he is to carry on this business in the future.

"Although in the order communicated by Your Excellency on the 31st of December '79 it is virtually commanded that to attract the Moquis they should be helped and satisfied, and as a consequence the royal treasury would meet the expenses occasioned thereby, it appears that Anza does not ask for his reimbursement, inasmuch as he confines his inquiry as to those arising in the future, in this matter as well as in that of giving presents and satisfying the heathen nations who keep themselves at peace; and not having any fund from which to draw, as there is none, the Garrison enjoying only its allowance, or having signified to the Company, according to regulations, that it is indispensable that the expenses for these purposes be obligatory and necessary, the contingent fund may furnish them, and lacking that, the royal treasury. So it appears to me that Your Excellency may allow it, ordering the governor to endeavor to avoid those that are not of acknowledged use or necessity, and that he must give an account and reason for those of this class that he may make, in order that Your Excellency may order their payment, according to your judgment; In spite of which Your Excellency will decide everything according to his pleasure:

Arispe July 29, 1780 —Galindo Navarro.

Arispe July 30, 1780—

As it appears to the Counsellor passing upon the accompanying official letter of Lieut -Colonel Don Juan Baupta de Anza—Decroix—

By your letter of the 26th of May last, I am informed of the number of Moquis you have succeeded in attracting to that Province and of the arrangements you are planning to induce the rest of the Nation to follow their example, which under-taking, through your efficiency, promises me favorable results

The indispensable expenses that it may be necessary to meet for those Indians, as well as for the savages who are keep-ing the peace, will be supplied from the contingent fund of that Garrison, you furnishing an account and itemized list of all those occasioned by this object, so that passing through my hands, I may authorize their proper reimbursement; but I must advise you to try and avoid all that are not of acknowl-edged use or unavoidable necessity because His Majesty wishes the greatest economy observed in the increased expenditures that these Provinces occasion to the Treasury.

God Grant You many years—Arispe July 30, 1780—

(To) Señor Don Juan Baupta de Anza—
"Señor Commandant General—

My Dear Sir: By the accompanying Diary Your Excel-lency will be advised of the reasons I had for going myself to the Province of Moqui, of the activity I exercised for the pur-pose of bringing its inhabitants voluntarily to the subjection of His Majesty, and their Misery and the State to which this Province is reduced; to which facts, further than I exhibit them in the Diary aforesaid, I will add what I think about them at the time I may have the honor of presenting myself be-fore you.

Our Lord keep Your Excellency many years   City of Santa Fee 9th of November 1780—M S. M   Your most de-voted and faithful Servant kisses your hand—

JUAN BAUPTᴬ DE ANZA.

Señor Mariscal de Campo Don Teodor de Croix—

Diary of the Expedition made into the Province of Moqui by the Undersigned Lieut. Colonel Governor and Commandant of New Mexico, in which are shown the classes of the Troops and Persons accompanying him for the purposes hereafter explained

List of the Troops, Fathers Superior and Indians who went on said Expedition:

	Officials	Fathers Superior	Sergeants	Corporals	Soldiers	Indians	Number
Garrison of Sta Fee	2	2	1	2	31	0	38
Fathers Superior		2					
Tegua Indians Converted ----------------						40	40
do Queres						40	40
do Moquis						8	8
	2	2	2	2	31	88	126

After having used, in the preceding year and in the commencement of the present, the diligence which I reported to my Superior Chief, the Señor Governor and Cammandant-General, for the benefit of the Province of Moqui,[19] with the

19 The Moqui occupy a group of pueblos in N E. Arizona. They are known among themselves as the Hopituh—which means the peaceful people. Both Cushing and Bandelier state that there is no doubt that the province of Totonteac, mentioned by Fray Marcos de Niza in 1539 is identical with the province of Tusayan, or the Hopi country visited in 1540, by command of Francisco Vasquez Coronado, by Pedro de Tobar, accompanied by the Fray Juan de Padilla and a few horsemen and foot-soldiers It was on this visit that Tobar learned of the existence of the Grand Canyon of the Colorado The next Spaniard to visit Moqui was Don Antonio de Espejo. They were known to him by the name of Mohace, consisting of five villages, of which Awatobi was the principal. The Hopi gave Espejo a lot of cotton kilts, for which they were celebrated.
,Following Espéjo came Don Juan de Oñate, who received their submission on November 15th, 1598. From his itinerary (Doc Inéd. de Indias, xvi, 274-275) it would seem that on the occasion of his visit there were only four of the Hopi pueblos, but in the "Memorial sobre el descubrimiento del Nuevo México y sus acontecimientos—Años desde 1595 á 1602" (Doc Inéd. de Indias xvi, 207) the following Hopi pueblos are mentioned·Aguato (Awatobi), Gaspe (Gualpe, Walpi), Comupavi (Shongopovi), Majanani (Mishongnovi), and Olalla (Orabi), which covers all of the pueblos occupied by this tribe for many years after the visit of Oñate.
From the Segunda Relacion of Fray Alonso de Benavides it appears that the expedition to found the missions at Moqui was organized at Santa Fe beginning June 23, 1629, on which date they left the capital of the Province, A part of the expedition reached Moqui August 20th, 1629, the other having been left at Zuñi and Ancoma The frayles who went to Moqui were Francisco de Porras. Andrés Gutierrez, Cristóval de la Concepción and Francisco de Buenaventura, who were accompanied by a detachment of twelve soldiers In 1680, at the time of the Pueblo revolution, according to Vetancur (Crónica, pp. 321-322) the missions of Hopi were San Bernardino de Ahuatobi, 26 leagues from Zuñi, pop 800, Fray José de Figueras (Figueroa), alias de la Concepción, native of Mexico killed in the rebellion San Bartolomé de Xongopabi (Shongopovi), 7 leagues further (at Middle Mesa), with Moxainabe (Mishongnovi) as a visita; large church, pop 500; José Trujillo, native of Cadiz, killed in the rebellion. San Francisco de Oraybe (Oraibi), toward the west, last monastery of Moqui, 14,000 gentiles before their conversion, but they were consumed by pestilence, "tenia en el una aldea llamada Gualpimas, de mil y doscientos personas," meaning that Gualpi (Walpi) was its visita with a population of more than 1,200 souls; P F Jose de Espeleta and P F. Agustin de Santa Maria were the missionaries murdered and the church was destroyed by fire. Awatobi was destroyed in

New Mexico Historical Society Collections.

TERRACED HOUSES, ZUÑI.

purpose of persuading its afflicted inhabitants that they should
try settlement in our Pueblos as the only means of saving themselves, thus following out their own pious end and with much
greater advantages the Royal and Superior orders which as a
result of the first one, my aforesaid Superior Officer was
pleased to communicate to me for my guidance, under date of
December 31 of the same year, in due observance and with re-
spect to the main spirit of them, I sent, on two occasions, con-
fidential emissaries to the Moquis themselves, so that through
their efforts those who wished to accept voluntarily the said
departure might advise me, on learning which they would be
brought with all possible comforts for those persons who might
be pleased to come.

To which they replied, on the 25th of August last past,
that at least 40 families would undertake it, on which condition
I personally went to bring them at the end of a month, for
which purpose I provided the supplies, people and horses
which I calculated would be required for their maintenance.

1700; owing to the attitude of the people to the other Hopi and the fact
that they had asked the Spaniards for missionaries, the natives fell upon
them before daybreak, killed many of the inhabitants, and distributed the
survivors among the other pueblos From that time Awatobi was abandoned, but the walls of the church of San Bernardino or San Bernardo,
are still standing to a height of several feet on Antelope Mesa.
    Frederick Webb Hodge, note 38, pp. 258-9 Fray Alonso de Benavides'
Memorial, says that "The pueblos of Walpi, Mishongnovi, Shongopovi, and
Oraibi do not occupy their sixteenth and seventeenth century sites at the
base of the mesas, but, following the revolt, doubtless in fear of Spanish
vengeance, built new towns on the summits, where they still stand."
During the revolt of 1680 and later, in 1694-6, many of the Rio Grande
pueblos fled to Hopi. "Some of these" continues Hodge "built the town
of Payupki on the Middle Mesa, but were brought back and settled at
Sandia in 1748." See The Spanish Archives of New Mexico, R E. Twitchell,
vol I, pp 235-6, as to the founding of this Spanish-built pueblo of Sandia
"About the year 1700," says Hodge, "the pueblo of Hano was established
on the East Mesa by Tewa from the Rio Grande, on the invitation of
the Walpi people Here they have lived uninterruptedly ever since, and although intermarried considerably with the Hopi, they retain their native
tongue and many of their distinctive rites and customs. Two of the pueblos,
Sichumovi on the East Mesa, and Shipaulovi on the Middle Mesa, are of com-
paratively modern origin, having been established about the middle of the
eighteenth century Thus the Hopi pueblos, or the Province of Tusayan,
today consist of. Walpi, Sichumovi, and Hano (frequently but improperly
called Tewa, the name of the people) on the East Mesa; Mishongnovi
Shupaulovi, and Shongpovi, on the Middle Mesa, and Oraibi on the West
or Oraibi Mesa. Within the last decade a small pueblo known as Hotavila
has sprung up west of Oraibi, having been built by the conservative ele-
ment of the Hopi of Oraibi who refused to send their children to the government school Also may be included in the Hopi pueblo group this
summer settlement of Moerkapi, northwest of Oraibi This village was
probably that mentioned in 1604 by Oñate under the name Rancho de los
Gándules (Doc. Inéd. de Indias xvi, p. 276), while Fr Francisco Garcés
(see Elliott Coues' translation of his Diary, N Y , 1900) referred to it in
1776 as Muqui concabe and Munqui concabe The total Hopi population
(including the Tewa of Hano) in 1910 was 1,941."
    Translated, Ranchos de los Gándules would mean the Ranch of the
Vagabonds or Wanderers—in modern slang—"Hobos."
    Neither Hodge, Bandelier, or any of the writers, so far as I have learn-
ed, mentioned the fact disclosed in this Diary that in 1780, also, and for a
few months prior, quite a large number of the Moqui left and joined the
Rio Grande Pueblos, except Bancroft, Arizona and New Mexico, p. 266).

safety and transportation, with all of which I undertook the expedition in the manner hereinafter described.

"Days—Sunday—10th of September, 1780, at six ' in the morning, I set out from the Villa (Santa Fe), in company with the Reverend Father Fray Sebastian Fernandez, and by the Royal Road (Camino Real),[20] in a Southerly direction, 12 leagues were made until our arrival at the Pueblo of San Phelipe.

Summary of Leagues—From Sta Fee to San Phe[21]—12 leagues Monday 11th—At seven in the morning I continued the march by the same road and in the same direction for three leagues to the Pueblo of Sta. Ana,[22] from which I inclined to

---

20   The Camino Real followed by de Anza was the old Santa Fe-Chihuahua Trail, the oldest highway in the United States. In an ancient archive, in my possession, undated, the stations on this trail are given as follows:—

Distancia de Santa Fe á Chihuahua

Los Tanques	12		S Diego	78	255
Juana Lopez	3	15	Roblerito	12	267
S Phelipe	18	33	Robledo	3	270
Algodones	3	36	Doña Ana	16	286
Bernalillo	6	42	Bracito	18	304
Sandia	4	46	Paso del Norte	33	337
Alameda	6	52	Ojo de Samalayucca	36	373
Alburquerque	12	64	Candelaria	24	397
Los Varelas	3	67	Ojo Lucero A S	15	412
Peralta	16	83	Laguna de Patos	12	424
Valencia	3	86	Carrizal	18	442
Tome	6	92	Ojo	12	454
Casa Colorada	9	101	Jesus Maria	21	475
Joya de Cebolleta	15	116	Lagantijan	15	490
Sabino	17	133	Chivato-desde del cerro	21	511
Parida	3	136	Gallego	12	523
Bosque de Luis Lopez	6	142	Laguna	37	550
Valverde	15	157	Penolito	30	580
Contadero	6	163	Sacramentito	33	613
Fray Cristobal	14	177	CHIHUAHUA	18	631

21   In 1591, Castaño de Sosa visited the pueblo of San Felipe and probably gave it its Saint name It formerly was located at the foot of the black mesa of Tamita, where they were visited by Coronado in 1540 Oñate also visited the place in 1598 The Franciscans established a seat here at an early date, the first church having been erected by Fray Cristóbal de Quiñones These Indians were active in the revolution of 1680 and helped to murder the frayles at Santo Domingo a few miles up the Rio Grande. After the Spaniards had been driven out and during Otermin's rule at El Paso, when he tried to re-conquer the lost territory (1681) they abandoned the pueblo and fled to the Potrero Viejo but returned in 1683 When General de Vargas made his first entrada (1692) they again fled to the Potrero but later were induced to return. In 1693, at the time of de Vargas' second entrada the Indians had built a new pueblo on top of the Mesa, immediately back of the present pueblo, and a little farther north In 1694, a church was built here, a part of the walls of which may still be seen on the very brow of the mesa. It was during the second term of De Vargas that the present village was built

22.   Frederick Webb Hodge, op. cit., note 25, p 226 says—"The original pueblo, according to Bandelier, stood near the Mesa del Cangelon, west of the Rio Grande and north of Bernalillo, but this was abandoned before the advent of the Spaniards in the sixteenth century, and another built, about midway between the present Santa Ana and San Felipe, on the great Black Mesa of San Felipe This was the village visited by Oñate in 1598, who referred to it as Tamy and Tamaya—the latter being the name applied by the inhabitants to both this pueblo and its predecessor It was early the seat of a Spanish mission, and although it had no resident priest at the time of the revolt, it was not without a church and monastery. In the revolt, the Santa Ana tribe joined the natives of San Felipe in the massacre of the priests at Santo Domingo and the colonists in the Rio

the west through a country little beaten down or trailed; at about eleven leagues I halted at the Rio Puerco[23] where I joined the Train of Supplies, carts and re-mounts that had set out from the Villa on the 8th.

From Sta Fee to the Rio Puerco—22 leagues.

Although upon our first arrival at this place several Indians of the Heathen Tribe of the Navajo Apaches had taken to flight, being recovered from their first suspicion and seeing that they were approached in a friendly way, two of them came to ascertain and remained the greater part of the night among us; on the following day they returned in company with one of their Captains and a dozen persons of both sexes, whom I exhorted to live peaceably, guaranteeing to them that with the preceding condition they should enjoy our Friendship always, after which I presented them with some tobacco.

Tuesday 12th—At quarter of seven our train was moving; by a little used trail and over the most broken Country they marched 10 leagues to the west; when we arrived at the pueblo of la Laguna,[24] where I was joined by the Rev. Father Fray Andrés Garcia, who is the Superior of the two who accompany me—

From Sta Fee to la laguna 32 leagues—

Wednesday 13th—A little after seven, by the royal road to the Pueblo of Suñi,[25] the route was followed in a Westerly Direction over a good country on which they marched six leagues until arrival at the neighborhood of Nacimiento—

Grande valley As the pueblo was situated west of the Rio Grande it was not molested by Governor Otermin during his attempt to reconquer New Mexico in 1681, but in 1687, Pedro Reneros de Posada, then Governor at El Paso, carried the pueblo by storm after a desperate resistance, and burned the village, several Indians perishing in the flames When de Vargas made his appearance in 1692 the tribe occupied a mesa known as Cerro Colorado, 10 miles to the north, and eastward from Jemez, but were induced to return to their former locality where they built the pueblo now occupied, and which like the two others, is known as Tamaya In 1782, Santa Ana was a visita of Sia Its population in 1910 was 211. See Bandelier, Final Report, pt i, p 126, pt. 2 p 193 et seq Bancroft, Arizona and New Mexico, p 200 et passim."

23. Near the place now called Cabezon.

24 This pueblo was built toward the close of the year 1697, it lies 17 miles northeast of Acoma on the Rio Cubero, the inhabitants are Queres descendants of rebellious members of that nation from the pueblos of Santo Domingo, Cochiti Sia and Acoma. Governor and Captain General Don Pedro Rodriguez Cubero, who succeeded General De Vargas, visited the place in 1699, when the natives declared their allegiance to the Spanish crown and the town was called San José de la Laguna, from the lagoon which formerly existed west of the pueblo

25. "From an historical point of view," says Hodge, "the present pueblo of Zuñi is one of the most interesting in New Mexico, since it is the survivor of one of the Seven Cities of Cibola discovered by Fray Marcos de Niza in 1539, and conquered by Francisco Vasquez Coronado

Photographed by Bradfield—Courtesy State Museum.

PUEBLO OF WALPAI.

From Sta Fee to Nacimiento 38 leagues—

Thursday 14th—At half past six the March was continued in the said direction making two leagues, over a broken country, after which, the latter improving, we continued three leagues more in the right direction and finished the Journey at the Paráje del Gallo.

From Sta Fee to el Gallo[26] 43 leagues—

Friday 15th—At six the Route was continued in a westerly direction over middling country in which lies the cañon and **sierra** of Suñi so-called through which we covered nine leagues until we arrived at La Tinaja—

From Santa Fee to la Tinaja 52 leagues—

Saturday 16th—At the same hour as on the preceding day, we began our march in the said direction over level country on which we covered six leagues until our arrival at Ojitto,[7] where our train remained till the following morning.

From Santa Fee to Ojitto 58 leagues—

The evening of this day I went to the Pueblo of Suñi, not only to attend to some matters of Justice for the natives, who, as they are the last and furthest to the West of the Province under my charge, seldom appeal to their Governor; but also, to learn of their condition and circumstances. Their existence I found to be most deplorable in every particular, owing to the lack of rain in these parts for the last two years, on which chance their comfort depends, as all the crops they make are temporal[28] and the failure of these has reduced the number of inhabitants to a very few, they being the most numerous in the Province, and the preceding (condition) requiring them to continue living at the ranches where they pasture their small stock, of which there is a reasonable abundance; and the others, a larger number, are in our interior pueblos, and are hoping that after the misfortunes they have suffered, the greater part of them may recover this present year through the abundant crops they now have, which will be harvested, if

in the year following. From the Spanish chroniclers of the sixteenth century considerable data of ethnologic and historical importance have been derived, and their descriptions are amply definite to leave no doubt of the identification of the so-called Seven Cities of Cibola with the pueblos inhabited by the Zuñi Indians at that time. These are now survived by the single village of Zuñi (so called from its Queres name) ….."

26 A very large spring near the present town of San Rafael. It has always been a "paraje" or stopping-place.

27. Now called Ojo del Pescado.

28. Dry-farming, without artificial irrigation

Divine Providence retards during this month the frosts that are accustomed to occur at this time

Sunday 17—Our train moved from the vicinity of Ojitto at six, and, marching to the west, over good country, six leagues to its finish, arrived at the pueblo of Suñi, where, stopping to water the horses, it rejoined me and with it we changed our direction to the Northwest, in which and over level country we made three leagues more and concluded the journey at the waterless region of las Pastorias.

From Sta Fee to la Pastoria 66 leagues—

Monday 18th—At six the route was continued over fairly good ground to the Northwest and, after making two leagues, we passed a fair watering place, from which we took our leave for another larger one, distant from the preceding six leagues more, and called la Casa.[29]

From Sta Fee to the watering-place of la Casa 75 leagues—

The evening of this day I ordered an Indian, trusted by me and acquainted with the Moqui language, well known to that Nation on account of commissions he has had from me and other governors, accompanied by four of his own Nation, who have submitted to us this present year, and by five older Christian (Indians) of equal understanding and intelligence, to announce to the inhabitants of the Country toward which we are marching our peaceful arrival within four days, and particularly to those who summoned us and besought that we might take them from the misery they are suffering, and to declare to them the benefits in which we will make them participants to all those who of their own free will wish to enjoy the same; which announcements, for their greater satisfaction, I offered to have repeated to them by one of the Reverend Fathers who accompany me prior to my entry into their pueblos, and for whose attention as well as for those maintaining order among them, I gave to the principal commissioner my share of rations and tobacco, in order that they might the more easily, and as is customary among them, inaugurate such conversions

Tuesday 19th—At twelve today in order later to reach water more easily, we returned to the trail which led to the Northwest over good country until we had made five leagues,

---

29 Northeast of San Rafael.

where we found abundant rain-water in a place called Las
Tinajas, and there we remained to pass the night.

From Sta Fee to la Tinaja[30] 80 leagues—

Wednesday 20th—At six we followed the route in the direction of west northwest, over fair ground, until we had covered four leagues, at the end of which we arrived at the Navajo
Spring, from which, having watered the horses, we continued
four leagues farther to a waterless plain.

From Sta Fee to the Waterless Plain 88 leagues—

Thursday 21st—At six we resumed our march over vary-
ing ground and in a direction west and northwest in such manner that eight leagues were consumed before we arrived at the
Gualpi Spring, which we found somewhat scant.

From Sta Fee to the Gualpi Spring 96 leagues—

For this reason and because it was necessary to remain
some days in these regions I caused search to be made in various directions in order to ascertain if rain-water could be located—this being the season for it—and they succeeded in
finding some at a distance of a little more than three leagues.

Friday 22nd—At six we took the road in a southerly direction to the place before-mentioned which we knew the
Natives call Aguattobi, which is known to have been peopled
by them long ago; there I determined to wait the result of the
mission of the emissaries. This place might be considered as
the chief pueblo of Moqui on account of what has been re-
lated, as well as because it is parallel with a similar inhabited
one now existing.

From Sta Fee to Vattovi (sic) 99 leagues—

At two in the afternoon some of the emissaries before mentioned returned bringing the news that they had been pleas-
urably received in all of the pueblos of their mission and that
most of their caciques told them they would be pleased to see
me there, but begging me not to force any of their people to
abandon their pueblos, seeing that most of them desired to end
their lives there, notwithstanding the misfortunes of war and
hunger which they were undergoing, and they added that the
forty families which had first summoned me, they had taken,
fifteen days before my departure (from Santa Fe) to await my
arrival in the country and possessions of the Navajo Apaches.

30 Here the Mazon family settled about 1866.

Photographed by Bradfield—Courtesy State Museum.

PUEBLO OF WALPAI.

believing that they would give them shelter as friends, as they had done at other times, they having previously offered it to them; believing which they had put themselves in their power, but these Barbarians had abused the Confidence which had been placed in their word, and had committed the treason of murdering all the men and making prisoners of the women and innocent children, which lamentable event was known through two of the former who had succeeded in making their escape and return to their country; but, notwithstanding this grievous accident, some persons had presented themselves, begging them to lead them to our territory, so that they might not remain to perish in their own.

Seeing that on this account my expedition was unsuccessful in its main object, I arranged, having failed in that, to find out at least the situation and circumstances of this Province in what might occur in the future, and likewise, to advise myself with certainty as to what would conduce to its better government, hoping, at the same time, that my presence might possibly succeed in attracting to our authority some more of the unhappy people.

In order to accomplish this, I immediately arranged, with the concurrence of the Reverend Fathers accompanying me, that one of them should go that same afternoon to the two principal pueblos and inform the chief cacique of them all—the cacique of Oraibe, that inasmuch as he had signified a desire to meet me the next day, that I would be with him, with the understanding that I would do nothing which might be contrary to his wishes, as I had repeatedly declared to all of them, nor need he have any fear as to anything else, inasmuch as I would be accompanied only by the number of troops and Indians indispensably necessary to guard me against our common enemies—the Apaches, with which commission, the said Father left the encampment, accompanied by four interpreters.

Saturday 23rd—Having decided that the present camp, where it has been since yesterday, should remain garrisoned with the major portion of the men, I set out therefrom at five in the morning for the purposes already stated, in company with an officer, the other Reverend Father, twenty troopers and fifteen Indians, with the Pueblo of Oraibe as my destination, the same being the capital of this Province of Moqui, situated to the northwest of the camp, eight leagues distant, in which passage I marched by the neighboring two remaining pueblos, meeting many of their inhabitants of both sexes, who saluted us joyfully, to whom we returned salutations with the addition of food and other gifts.

At eleven I arrived at the pueblo of Oraibe, and its Cacique having received me with some perturbation of spirit, although in the presence of all his people, and encouraged by the Father and the interpreters who had already told him that I was there to reassure him, and when I came up, I told him

That the Most Pious Sovereign and the Great Chief, whom I have the honor to serve and obey, expected nothing further of him, and of all who are unfortunate in being separated from his dominion, than this—that they should above all, recognize as the true God, the Creator of man, of the Heavens, and of the Sun, and of all that is visible, and to recognize also His Majesty as their King and Master, it being understood that the one and the other recognition must be voluntary and that as a result thereof, neither he nor any one else would lose his command and the dignity and dominion of a Cacique, but, on the contrary, his authority and liberty would be the greater in all justice; that His Majesty, being in the highest degree just, as he is pious, if they still did not care to become his vassals, he would not compel them, and so that they may not fail in receiving the benefits thereby occasioned, I offer them our friendship and trade with the assurance that they will be treated with the greatest kindness and to their satisfaction

To all of which he made reply that he and all of his great Nation have recognized and known as their Lord and King him whom the Spaniards have as such, relinquishing their own; as to God, although they have not received the Water of Baptism, they also turn to his Divine Majesty in their present afflictions, although they had almost decided as they were consulting me —and he testified that they had decided because he saw that of his small tribe, the greater number were still in a heathen state—he had resolved to die with those who remained, in their own way, with the exception of those who might care to follow me in order to become Christians, with whom, so far as he was concerned, he would not interfere either now or in the future. As to establishing trade, he was most grateful on that score and that they would take advantage of my offer to carry it on in our country if some day they succeeded in re-establishing themselves, although he believed that impossible because of the extermination of his Nation and the loss of their lands for lack of rain and fertility in parts, and in addition the continual war made upon them by the Utes and Navajos, about whom he complained bitterly, relative to my object in offering to mediate between the two nations; that his people were more determined now, great as had been their determination in the past, all of which they had previously informed me, and he told me that I should let the matter stand as it was, inasmuch as he had made up his mind to die at the hands of his enemies.

Notwithstanding all this, I made offers to this Cacique that by going or sending to my encampment I would make him gifts for the relief of his present necessities, of a horse loaded with food, which, however, he would not accept pretending that he had nothing to offer in return, since without such reciprocity, their customs would not permit it.

After having spent considerable time in conversation about other matters not disagreeable to this individual, I returned to the question of religious matters, adding that if he cared to hear about them, the Reverend Father who accompanied me would tell him with the greatest pleasure, to which he quickly replied that he did not care to hear them at all, with which last refusal, and assuring me that he would keep peace with us, I concluded to leave him with no other success than a refusal of the merciful and gentle means by which the knowledge of both Powers could be gained whenever he desired it, as also for his people who have asked him for help and protection in the time of their greatest calamity and when all the Nations of their kind are conspiring for the total destruction of the few remaining, in continual proof that my Catholic King and Honorable Superior have no other end in view than to bestow upon him the greater part of their possessions, both spiritual and temporal and with which their Christian desires might be superabundantly satisfied.

With this last conversation, which, to my thinking, convinced all of those present, although it did not alter their determination (because that is reserved for Divine Providence) I left this Pueblo, leaving to the Reverend Father (to take)

Photographed by Bradfield—Courtesy State Museum.
PUEBLO OF WALPAI.

the road to Walpi, with a sufficient escort of our men, in order
that he might let the other people know that those who were
willing to submit to our care and follow us could come to him,
with which understanding, I returned at nine at night to my
encampment

Sunday 24th—I waited in order that the aforesaid people
might come together and learned at the end of the afternoon
that they were thirty in all, for whom I ordered sufficient
horses, with orders that they join me tomorrow afternoon at
the Gualpi Spring

This morning a considerable number of Moquis, the larger
part from Oraibe, came to our camp, asking for the opening
of trade, which I granted to them, with advantages they have
never before experienced; for which reason they consorted
with us so much that even after they had finished, they remained throughout the entire day.

Inasmuch as we were in this Province called Moqui, which
with its population has always been considerable in these regions of the interior, it does not seem to me out of place to
compare the state in which it was during the year just recently
passed, 1775, when it was exactly and accurately investigated
by the Reverend Father Silvestre Veles Escalante,[31] and its
present condition, in order that its frightful desolation may
be known, though it must be said that the natives themselves
declare that it commenced since '77

The said Reverend Father, in his aforesaid inquiry, reports that the Province of Moqui consists of seven pueblos containing the following families; the first 110, the second 15, the
third 200, the fourth 50, the fifth 14, the sixth 60 and the
seventh 800, the total of which amounts to 1249, and of persons, 7494. The livestock, large and small, he does not give at
a fixed number, but by common report, there are in all this
Province about 300 sheep and many cattle [32]

Today, the seven pueblos are reduced to five; the first
and second have 40 families, the third 45, the fourth 10 and the

---

31   The Spanish Archives of New Mexico, R E Twitchell, vol. II,
p 259, Archive 704; p 267, Archive 779

32   In relation to this expedition of Fr Escalante, with references to
his Informe y Diario, see Arizona and New Mexico p 261 and note, H
H Bancroft See also On the Trail of A Spanish Pioneer, the diary and
itinerary of Franco Garcés, containing extracts from Escalante's Diario-
Elliott Coues, New York, Harper, 1900, v 2 pp 366 and 469 See also
note, 13 ante, as to map of Moqui

fifth, the Capital, Oraive, 38 to 40, which by the usual rule
(which cannot now be applied) of six persons to a family
would make the preceding 133 families equal 738 persons,
which is the most as will be found true, from which it follows
that in the three years previously noted, 6698 have died. But
they concealed from us that among the pagan nations friendly
to them they have some horses; they assured us they have no
more than five head in all the pueblos, no cattle and about
300 sheep, the greater number of which we saw in the Pueblo
of Gualpi. The crops they now have are numerous, but have
done badly as much on account of being in sandy soil as because it has not rained; so that we calculate they will not har-
vest altogether two hundred bushels of all grains.

The causes which have contributed to the extermination of
these pueblos or the Province, including all its natives, have
been hunger and pestilence, the first because it has not rained
since the year '77, and from that has resulted the second, to
which may be added the war cruelly made upon them by the
Utes and Navajos, there is not lacking to the aforesaid
(causes) another which appears supernatural, which, although
they did not tell it to me,(they did tell it to many of the Indians of my company who have submitted, with them they
talked with greater confidence;) which is that the said calamities came upon them because of the ill-treatment and contempt
bestowed by them in the past year of '76 upon the venerable
Apostolic Father Fray Francisco Garzes. They declare that
not having wished to hear the gospel preached which he tried
to give them, he prophesied to them that they would not escape the aforesaid miseries which they are experiencing, for
which reason they now praise him, which I consider this
zealous man of Religion has always deserved

Prior to the aforesaid, my limited consideration could only
marvel that the Province or Pueblos spoken of had existed so
many years in the power that the old chronicles demonstrate,
not as we see it today in the last stages of extermination, because of which the most fundamental things are wanting for
its preservation since in the four leagues or a little more in
which the crops are situated, there is no living water with
which to irrigate ten bushes of any plant whatever, what they
call fields are sand-heaps which consequently require double

rains; water for the people and animals for drinking purposes is extremely scanty and mostly dammed up, each person using his own As to timber and wood the condition is not to be wondered at, as favorable rains have failed for a few years and that accounts for the falling off in the abundance which usually occurs, and as to the natives, under these conditions, we are witnesses, as I certify, if they continue, it is their final destruction without hope that they may recover by other means, because all the country which I have travelled is waterless and the lands without indication of minerals or any other useful and valuable natural product with the exception of the limitless pit-coal which we[33] found in the middle of the day's march that was made on the 21st

Monday 25th—At twelve o'clock I began my return which as it was by the same places and marches is not described, unless some event occurred calling for special mention.

At five in the afternoon of this day, the Reverend Father Superior joined me with those who had voluntarily submitted, as described the day before, in whose company came the Cacique of the Pueblo of Gualpi, who, after having greeted me with the greatest demonstrations of affection, told me that their Supreme Cacique of Oraibe had come to see him the night before and informed him what I had said to him, and that he showed plainly that he was not inclined to accept any part of my proposals, to which he added that he had replied that notwithstanding his orders, the largest pueblo of his Nation was now disposed to go and live with him among the Spaniards, if their misfortunes continued, because it was less of a misfortune to perish in their country which did not afford them anything upon which to subsist, and that he himself was inclined to permit the whole of his tribe to be aided with knowledge and experience; that the Spaniards only desired their well-being, with which belief, in the presence of the Father, who was an onlooker, he had proclaimed to his people that they were free to follow us as many had wished to do.

In view of the reasonableness of this man. I showed him my pleasure and on that account I made him acquainted with all that I had said to him at Oraibe, in order that he, with all

33 This is the earliest mention of the immense coal deposits in New Mexico which I have found in any of the archives.

Photographed by Bradfield—Courtesy State Museum.
TRAIL TO ORAIBI.

his tribe, might reflect upon it; I offered to mediate with their enemies, the Utes and Navajoes that they might be permitted to live in peace, and, lastly, I impressed upon him that he and all others must understand that they will be admitted on the terms I have signified at any time whatsoever, to which reply I added the gift of a horse loaded with provisions and other charms (literally—"witchcraft"), with which he was most content, passing the night in our company

Tuesday 26th to Friday 29th—We passed in reaching the Pueblo of Suñi, during which period no event occurred worthy of mention

Saturday 30th—Having finished the matters which come up in the pueblo, I set out this day and passed the night in the vicinity of La Tinaja.

Sunday October 1st to Friday 5th--Were spent in reaching the Villa of Santa Fee

JUAN BAUPTᴬ DE ANZA

With your official letter, No 191, of the Ninth of November last, I received the Diary of the Journey Your Honor made to Moqui advising of the methods used for the voluntary reduction of these people I request Your Honor to tell me what you have to say concerning the inhabitants in order that, with this information, I may finish the report, giving account to His Majesty

God Preserve Your Honor many years. Arispe January 12 1780—

Señor Don Juan Bᵗᵃ de Anza.

My Dear Sir.—In Compliance with what Your Excellency is pleased to command under date of the 12th current, in regard to the people of the Province of Moqui, I state·

That what appears to me most in conformity with the pious intentions of His Majesty, prompted by Humanity, inasmuch as it leads to a good opinion of the Spanish Nation among all the Heathen, is that those who are in question be left to their present and ancient mode of living, so long as they do not accept the conditions which have been proposed to them: that those who have recently and voluntarily wished to submit to us be quickly supplied with assistance, that although this has only been moderate until now, it may be further reduced, if Your Excellency, in the matter of food supplies, will condescend to have them supplied out of what is produced in the several communities, particularly from those where they have been located and established, since these, owing to the benefits accruing on account of the increase (in population) have freely given them land, houses, livestock and other useful things with which to subsist, it is not to be doubted can contribute the above, which amounts to less. I am persuaded that the administration which I suggest is not only conducive in its results to the good of these people, but I deem it to be urgent, necessary and fitting in circumstances which are unfavorable to us; which are that the Navajo Apaches, who are their nearest neighbors, may increase by additions from these Moquis, since the former, having been our declared enemies, it is to be presumed that they would care to again become such, when they realize their size and growth, as our experience with every Indian tribe which considers itself numerous has tended to prove.

The Navajo Indian tribe, both by warlike acts and by the other deeds of violence which I have described, have secured many of the Moquis, of whom I am persuaded are to be included many more than have been told us, as also by similar conduct among themselves, in which case and in order to cut short the objects they have in view, it seems to me opportune that we exert ourselves by means which Your Excellency thinks best to order, so that those who may be opposed to us, may submit themselves to the happy control of His Majesty, although repugnant to them, which will soon pass away when the contentment we offer them has been demonstrated—the same contentment which something like two hundred persons of these very people whom we have converted are now enjoying, and of whom not one has returned to his old country.

Concerning which matters this is as much as I will allow myself to call to Your Excellency's attention, in order that above all you may deign to continue (to advise) me in whatever shall be your best pleasure, in all of which I shall enjoy the satisfaction of obeying your commands.

Our Lord Preserve Your Excellency many years   Arispe January 17th, 1781. M. S. M.   Your most devoted servant kisses your hand.

JUAN BAUP^TA DE ANZA.

Señor Caballero de Croix-Arispe January 20, 1781—
To the Counsellor· De Croix—

With your letter No. 208 I have sent the report upon the conversion of the Province of the Moqui to the Counsellor of the General Commandancia, deferring my decision with a view of (having) his opinion thereon

In the interim Your Honor will proceed in the matter according to your known zeal and experience and so that your actions may dissipate the ill feelings of the Navajos and soften those of the Moquis by attracting them to the service of God and the King through kindness and gentleness, and in no manner by severe measures which may hurt and exasperate them

God keep Your Honor many years   Arispe January 20, 1781—

Señor Don Juan B^ta de Anza.
Señor Commandant General:

The Governor Don Juan Baup^ta de Anza having stated in his last report of the 17th January of this year, that the gentle methods adopted by Your Excellency for the reduction of the Moquis and leading them to take up their residence in our settlements in New Mexico and re-people that Province, have produced the favorable effect of bringing into it voluntarily more than two hundred persons, who consider themselves happy on account of the reception and welcome which has been given to them, without caring to return to their old country where of necessity they fear that war, hunger and pestilence will pursue and annihilate them, as has been their experience in former years, it follows that in order to be successful in the conversion and voluntary conquest of a large number of those unfortunates, the same method is to be continued that has produced such excellent and favorable results, the performance of which should be entrusted to the same Governor, warning him to have particular care that those who submit shall fulfill the promises which they have made, that no injuries, vexations, insults or annoyances shall be caused them which would fret them and compel them to leave the pueblos where they have been concentrated and where they prefer the misfortunes they have suffered in their own rather than endure any which may be brought upon them

in their new homes   This may well be (done) from the contingent fund in the manner in which he was advised on the
30th of July of the year just past, or from the communities of
the pueblos as he proposes, or finally by other means which
his prudence and recognized judgment may determine, he
may arrange that to those already converted gifts may be
made of such aid and comfort as may be possible, so that
their condition being improved, and their subsistence and
that of their families having been assured, their own good
fortune being experienced and made known, these will consti-
tute the most vivid, attractive and efficacious examples, so
that the remainder of their Nation who remain obstinate in
their own pueblos, may accept the proposals to leave and
follow them voluntarily for the enjoyment of similar good
fortune, that to this end, from among those converted and
from among the other Indians whom he may consider the
most adapted for the enterprise, he arrange that under pre-
text of trade, some trusty emissaries, possessing his greatest
confidence, go soon to the Moqui pueblos and subtly spreading
among the Heathen the happiness they have enjoyed through
having joined our pueblos, where they lack for nothing and
are treated with the greatest humanity, they may proceed in-
sensibly stimulating a desire to follow them, and for that
reason they may seek the same conversion and addition to our
pueblos; and finally, in order to preclude any disappointment
as to the subsequent advantages, which they might compare
with the present unfortunate continuance with the Moquis.
let him also arrange that those who are converted and those
who may be converted, shall not be added to one pueblo, nor
to those which may be reasonably near-by, because besides
(the fact) that the charge of contributing to the aid and
comfort of so many new colonists would be excessively heavy,
he must in time guard against the danger that, being re-
united, or inclined to join together, they might easily agree to
return to their native soil, so soon as they see that the unfortunate conditions which obliged them to abandon it have improved, which will not be so easy for them to arrange or
carry out if dispersed and joined to many pueblos of the
Province, and particularly if they can be located and furnished with means to live in the most interior (pueblos) and dis-

tant from the confines of both provinces, in the attainment
of which you should charge the Governor that he pay the
most specific attention, taking such measures as in his dis-
cretion seem most opportune, or as Your Excellency may of
course decide relative to the entire matter, as may be your
pleasure.

Arispe, April 30, 1781—

GALINDO NAVARRO

Arispe, May 29, 1781—

As the Counsellor reports, let a copy of his opinion be
sent with the official letter to the Governor of New Mexico—
DE CROIX.

Señor Commandant General.

My Dear Sir Together with Your Excellency's Superior
Order of the 28th of May last past, I received the opinion of
his Counsellor General relative to the treatment which ought
to be accorded to the Moqui Indians who have submitted, in
the spirit of which I shall conform all my measures according
to what Your Excellency is pleased to advise, and having carried it into effect by sending on two occasions faithful and
intelligent messengers in order to learn whether some of them
cared to join us, no good result has followed, because for five
months they have been experiencing a bad epidemic of smallpox, which, according to what they inform me, will almost result in the final extermination of this unhappy Nation, in
which the wars made upon them by the pagan Utes and
Navajoes co-operates, having no arbiter to intervene for
them; unless this, indeed, may bring about their submission
to our pueblos, may Your Excellency understand that I shall
neglect no effort for the spiritual and temporal good which
may follow.

Our Lord keep Your Excellency many years

Santa Fee November 15, 1781—M. S. M. Your most de-
voted faithful servant kisses Your Excellency's hand.

JUAN BAUPTᴬ DE ANZA

Señor Marescal de Campo Teodoro de Croix.

Relative to what your Honor refers to in your official
letter of November 11th last, No. 243, concerning the state of
the Moqui Nation, I repeat that the occasions are to be improved which shall present themselves for reducing them by